Happy birthday,
Lynn. You'll love this!
Much love,
T, M, J, M, C + C
x   2014

Tales From When I Were A Lad ...

Tales From When I Were A Lad …

Andrew Davies

PORTICO

First published in the United Kingdom in 2013 by
Portico Books
10 Southcombe Street
London
W14 0RA
An imprint of Anova Books Company Ltd

© Anova Books 2013

This edition published in 2013 for Index Books

Original concept by Frank Hopkinson, Dicken Goodwin
and Jo Heygate

ISBN 13: 978-1-909396-22-7

A CIP catalogue record for this book is available from
the British Library.

10 9 8 7 6 5 4 3 2 1

Reproduction by Rival Colour Ltd.
Printed and bound by 1010 Printing International Limited, China

This book can be ordered direct from the publisher.
Contact the marketing department, but try your bookshop first.

www.anovabooks.com

Page 2: The last known photo of Colin Olthwaite.

Contents

We Were Always In Street

When I were a lad our parents always knew where we were.
Playing outside in street.
Ah, the fun you could have pushing a cardboard
box around all day.

Or attacking your neighbours.

Or standing on your head on the Withenshawe Road using your X-ray vision to stare into sewers.

Most accidents happen in the home,
so we were much safer outside lugging rocks.

You could sit on a road junction
for hours and not be disturbed.

If you wanted to be la-di-da, you could make yourself a sun-lounger.

Or revel in the luxury of your own crazy golf course.

Or crash and burn Mr Heptinstall's
new lawn mower.

We Craved Excitement

When I were a lad everything were boring.
Trainspotting the 9.53 from Hebden Bridge
were the height of excitement.

So if you got the chance to do something risky
you didn't think twice.
Like delivering fires to old people.

25

Soon you found your own way of cocking a snook at the accident statistics.

It may have risked sudden death or horrible injury,
but at least it weren't stamp collecting.

29

There were no pneumatic clamps,
safety bars or 'maximum capacity' on
old-fashioned thrill rides - you squeezed in...
...and occasionally out.

Trips to the zoo just weren't the same without a visit to Clive the clumsy elephant.

Still, you have to look up to your betters – and if they were risking it...

Thanks to Queen Mary we got Elizabeth II in 1952. If she hadn't been so careful it would have been Margaret I.

We Loved A Trip To Seaside

One of the biggest treats was a day trip to the seaside.
In those days you had a window you could gurn out of
and vomit from.

There were big arguments
about who got the spade.
Nothing changes...

No need for sun cream, the best you could hope for was a couple of 'bright intervals'.

For lunch, Auntie Violet would lower you
down the cliff for a gourmet feast
of fresh seagull eggs.

Washed down with a bucket of Chateau Bridlington '47.

Or Eau de Municipal Gardens.

Followed by a relaxing paddle.

A quick look at some donkey droppings.

And perhaps a bit of yachting.
We never quite got to Calais…

Grub

Food were awful. I'd like to see Jamie Oliver make
something interesting out of dinners at
Gasworks Lane Infants. There were no sun-dried
tomatoes in Mrs Bagshawe's mince.
Just good old-fashioned horses.

You were just grateful to have food.
Come sandwich time you'd want to eat
three or four at once.

That's if your thieving pooch didn't get to them first.

Dogs are supposed to be man's best friend,
but any opportunity...

Back then there was none of your Rocky Road
or Double Chocolate Chip Brownies.
We were in heaven at the sight of
fairy cakes with icing.

Or if we were really lucky –
milk and a root vegetable.

This Sporting Life

Olympic legacy? Back then we didn't even have a District Sports legacy. Our school long jump pit was in a builder's yard.

The swimming pool wasn't Olympic-sized,
it was reservoir-shaped.

High jump landing pit were a bit of loosened earth.

And our bikes weren't a patch on the ones ridden by those fancy continentals.

Ah, that glorious sound of summer...
rubber on packing crate.

Understanding Grown-ups

When I were a lad you didn't realise what
adults were up to half the time.

Innuendo passed you right by.
The ice cream man could say something like –
"that's sixpence love, have you got
a nice couple of threepenny bits" –
and you'd be none the wiser.

Sometimes you had no idea what they were saying at all.
But you grinned at them to keep them happy.

You were pretty sure King Neptune wasn't a real king and wasn't worshipped by fishes and all the creatures of the deep ocean. But you weren't going to argue.

But when Father Christmas told you to shove off and let him have his dinner in peace — that was a surprise.

Things Were Rubbish

When I was a lad so much of your life were rubbish.
The 'swan' on the municipal lake were rubbish.
Even if it were a duck it were rubbish.

The puppet shows they put on at school were rubbish.

The carnival float of the R100 Airship were rubbish.

And smelly, swotty Nigel said all your comics
were 'historically inaccurate'.

Posh kids could afford things that weren't rubbish.
Our boat cost us 2'6.

Marmaduke's scale model of the
Empress of India cost 14 guineas.

Posh kids looked so pleased with themselves,
posing with their model coaches and their model trains.
"...locomotives, actually."

And only a posh kid would go into space in a bow tie...

Animals Were Strange

When I were a lad they seemed
to make cats much bigger.

102.

They were like dogs –
except they were cats.

Simon Smith had this amazing bear.
Who'd have thought a boy and bear
could be well accepted everywhere.
It's just amazing how fair folks
can be.

Although nobody liked
Billy Holroyd's monkey. He always covered up
the good bits in magazines.

And our Beryl never forgave Dad for telling her
she might be fed to elephant if she were bad.

We Did This Stuff
Years Ago

People go on about new trends and new styles.
We had all this years ago. The low-slung crotch were
THE look, especially if you'd scored some gobstoppers.

We pioneered the bobble hat.

We had our own 'Disneyland'. You could find it in
Skegness, Clacton, Filey, Pwllheli, Bognor
and Barry Island.

We had people carriers.

We had yummy mummies jogging with their cross-country prammies.

We had poncey designer 'rooms in the garden' with 'vintage' crockery.

They hadn't invented global warming but that didn't stop us having the worst floods since records began.

And the worst droughts since records began.

There Was A First Time For Everything

You always remember the first time you did lots of things. The first time you bought your own fireworks.

Your first pagan ritual.

The first time you were served by royalty.
Strange that Prince Charles and Suggs
from Madness went to same school…

133

The first time she said she was your 'gal'

...then five minutes later said she preferred the dog.

Your first Bob-a-Job week.
Which fitted in neatly with your
first trip to a casualty department.

Your first fire drill.
Mr. Ormsby, the physics teacher, was out last
so we just let go.

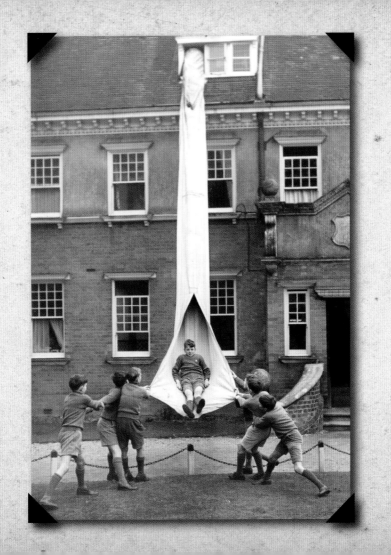

The first time you saw your dad with an inflatable crocodile on his head.

And the first time you really wanted
a pigeon to xxxx on someone!

Picture Credit Where
Picture Credit's Due

Other books in the series:

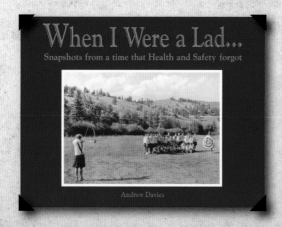

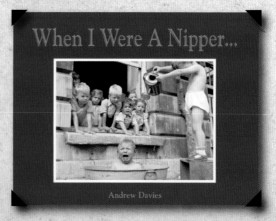